just

A LITTLE BOOK OF PIQUANT PLEASURES

PEPPERS.

The Editors of Lyons Press

Lyons Press
Guilford, Connecticut

An imprint of Globe Pequot Press

Copyright © 2011 by Morris Book Publishing, LLC

Lyons Press is an imprint of Globe Pequot Press.

Library of Congress Cataloging-in-Publication Data is available on file.

ISBN 978-1-59921-940-0

The information in this book is true and complete to the best of our knowledge. All recommendations are made without guarantee on the part of Globe Pequot Press. Globe Pequot Press disclaims any liability in connection with the use of this information.

Printed in China

10 9 8 7 6 5 4 3 2 1

CONTENTS

Bring on the heat!

Chile peppers were first cultivated in the early days
of the ancient Aztec Indians, when they were used to
flavor their diet of corn and beans. In modern dishes
they are not only used as a seasoning, they are also
stuffed and served as a main dish. As Tex-Mex and
Mexican food has become more popular in this coun-
try, the use of chiles, both dried and fresh, has soared.

Chiles come in many shapes and sizes and there
are over one hundred varieties from the mild sweet
bell to the fiery habañero. The heat from the chile
comes from a substance called capsaicin that is found
in the flesh and concentrated in the seeds and the
white veins that run inside the chile. Removing them
will remove some of the heat. Chiles are "rated"
according to the Scoville scale, developed by Wilbur
Scoville in 1912. He measured how much sugar it
takes to dilute the heat of peppers. The mildest peppers are sweet bell peppers, with no capsaicin. As the
peppers get hotter, the Scoville number increases,
going up to 15 million. That means the chiles have
to be diluted with 300,000 units of sugar before the

capsaicin can't be detected. The heat is detected by pain receptors in the tongue, which are located slightly under the surface. That's why it takes a few seconds for a chile's heat to register when you take a bite of hot and spicy food.

But chiles aren't just about heat. They have complex flavors, especially when roasted. Fresh chiles have a sweet undertone, and roasted chiles taste smoky and rich. Dried chiles taste smoky too, with a slightly spicy flavor.

So whether you prefer a more tame chile flavor or you seek the thrill of a spicy feast, *Just Peppers* will have *just* the recipe for you ●

TYPES OF PEPPERS

BELL PEPPERS

Is there a more perfect ingredient? Bell peppers are crisp, aromatic, and sweet and come in beautiful, bright colors. They are an excellent source of vitamin C and vitamin A, two antioxidants that help fight the free radicals that can lead to cholesterol buildup in the arteries. In addition, they contain beta-carotene, which, among other things, can help prevent cataracts.

Bell peppers are the only capsicum fruit that does not contain capsaicin, which puts the heat in peppers. Different types of bell peppers impart different flavors. Green peppers are unripe bell peppers and so have a slightly more bitter taste. Red, yellow, and orange peppers are sweeter. Always remove the seeds and inner ribs, which can be bitter, before adding bell peppers to dishes.

GREEN CHILES

Green chile season is considered to be late summer through fall, when most of the chiles planted in spring have matured and are ready to be harvested. They

come in many shapes and sizes and retain their color and flavor fairly well when canned. Although they are not quite as flavorful as fresh green chiles, their canned substitutes are pretty close in flavor and texture.

Green chiles are roasted and peeled before use. They are often seeded and then stuffed with cheese or a meat filling, or they are diced and used as a flavoring.

RED CHILES

The difference between green and red chiles is simply that red chiles are fully ripened and tend to be hotter.

Red chiles come in many shapes and sizes. They are often strung together on a rope to make ristas, which can be hung in the kitchen to allow the chiles to dry out and make them easy to access.

When they are dried, red chiles can take on a wrinkled appearance or may maintain a smooth skin. Dried red chiles are often ground into a powder for seasoning.

You can find dried chiles at many major grocery store chains in plastic cellophane bags near the other Mexican herbs and spices. Another option is to order

them online. Dried chiles can last over a year, so make sure to stock up.

When you buy dried chiles, look for a deep color and firm texture. The chiles should be firm but not brittle or hard. If they are slightly pliable, that's just fine.

You can grind dried chiles to make your own chile powder or paste (be careful to protect your eyes!) or you can soak them in hot water for ten to fifteen minutes. Remove the stems and mince or chop the chiles before use.

GUAJILLOS

Guajillo chiles are very popular in Mexico and are a major part of the chile-farming industry. They are usually found as dried pods that can be ground into guajillo chile powder or made into a chile paste. They have a reddish brown color and are well suited to almost any recipe that calls for dried chiles.

Guajillos require a long soaking time because they are tough and leathery. Guajillos are a great ingredient for salsa because they have a lot of rich, smoky flavor and they are not overly spicy. To select guajillo chiles, look for dried chiles that have a uniform dark reddish brown color. The chiles should be intact without any tears or holes. Avoid chiles with any light spots, as they may indicate mold or fungus. Dried guajillos should be tough and pliable, not brittle.

HABAÑEROS

The habañero chile is one of the spiciest in the world. It typically has a bright orange color, but can sometimes have a red or yellow hue. Habañero chiles originated in the Yucatan Peninsula region of Mexico thousands of years ago and are still widely used to season and flavor a variety of dishes. When the Europeans discovered the spicy chile, they brought it back to their homelands and its popularity quickly spread beyond Europe and into Asia.

If you can get past the fiery heat the habañero provides, you can begin to enjoy the subtle fruity flavors. Because of their fruit flavors, habañeros are delicious in salsas.

JALAPEÑOS

Jalapeños are small green chiles that are quite hot. They are often pickled with other vegetables such as

onions or carrots. The pickled versions are usually
used in recipes, but they can also be used as a condiment. Pickled jalapeños have a very strong jalapeño
flavor that is often desired in jalapeño-flavored recipes.

To deseed jalapeños, cut them in half lengthwise
and, with a paring knife, scrape out the seeds and
ribs. Since this is what gives jalapeños their spiciness,
the heat level will be drastically cut down.

When jalapeños are smoke-dried they are called
chipotles.

POBLANOS

Poblano chiles are named after the Mexican state of Puebla, which is where they originated. They are popular because they are large and sturdy enough to be stuffed with fillings. They are also readily available, making them an easy choice when green chiles are

Chiles and Scoville Units

Sweet bell peppers	0
Pepperocini	200
Coronado	800
Poblano	1,500
Ancho	1,500
Pasilla	1,800
Mirasol	3,000
Jalapeño	4,000
Chipotle	6,000
Serrano	10,000
Tabasco	40,000
Cayenne	50,000
Piquin	55,000
Thai	70,000
Bird's eye	150,000
Habañero	180,000
Scotch bonnet	200,000
Naga Jolokia	1,000,000
Pure capsaicin	15,000,000

called for. Poblanos are usually 4 to 6 inches in length and dark green in color. The heat of a poblano can vary greatly from very mild to medium hot. When poblanos are dried, they are referred to as ancho chiles.

SERRANOS

Serrano chiles are quite a bit hotter than jalapeños and are a bit smaller in size. Depending on the heat level you wish, they can pretty much be used interchangeably. Serranos can vary in color and are typically eaten raw.

ROASTING CHILES

Most recipes call for roasted chiles. When you roast a chile, you char it and remove the skins, adding flavor. You can roast a chile over an open flame, on a comal or griddle, in a broiler, or on a grill. Chiles can be roasted whole or cut in half. On the broiler, it's easier to roast if they are cut in half. Rinse the chiles and pat dry, then place on the grill or broiler pan, or skewer on a long skewer for cooking on an open flame. Char until the skin is black and blistered. Then place the chile in a plastic bag, paper bag, or covered

bowl for 10–15 minutes to build up steam that will loosen the skin. The skin will be easy to peel off and the seeds and veins can be scraped out. Never rinse chiles that have been roasted and peeled; you'll rinse away all of the flavor you built.

WORKING WITH HOT CHILES

Use care when working with fresh, canned, or dried chiles. The capsaicin in chiles is the same ingredient used in pepper spray and is what causes them to burn unprotected skin and eyes. The chemical is concentrated in the white veins and seeds, so to reduce the heat, remove these from the chiles. Wear latex gloves when handling hot chiles to avoid soaking fingertips in pepper oils and keep your hands away from your eyes, lips, or other mucus membranes before thoroughly washing your hands in soapy water.

REHYDRATING CHILES

To rehydrate a chile, cut the stem off, make a slit down the side, and remove the seeds and veins. Place the chiles in a bowl of hot water and let soak about 30 minutes. When softened you can use the chiles as

desired. If the soaking liquid is not overly bitter, use a couple of tablespoons to blend the chiles into a paste, or use the liquid in place of water needed in a recipe.

CHOOSING AND STORING CHILES

Your local farmers' market or Latin market is probably the best place to find fresh chiles. Fresh chiles should be firm and brightly colored, with no soft spots or wet spots. They should smell fresh and not have any mold or mildew around the stem. Do not purchase chiles with dark spots; they could be infected with fungus. If heat level is a concern, there is no way to tell from the outside what it will be. Sometimes a grocer or farmer can advise you, but even that can be unreliable because everyone's heat perception is different. You can soak the chiles in cool water for 30 minutes to help reduce the heat level. Fresh chiles will keep in the refrigerator for five to six days if in a crisper or plastic bags.

You can find dried chiles in the international foods aisle of most large supermarkets, or in ethnic grocery stores. The chiles should be dry but not brittle. They should still be pliable, and be free of mold or wet spots ●

Jalapeño-Paneer Poppers

INGREDIENTS

3 garlic cloves, minced
1 tablespoon vegetable oil
200 grams paneer, grated
¼ teaspoon red chile powder
½ teaspoon coriander powder
½ teaspoon cumin
½ teaspoon garam masala powder
2 tablespoons tomato paste
Salt, to taste

10 jalapeños, halved and deseeded
2 eggs, beaten
1½ cups bread crumbs
Oil, for deep-frying

YIELD: 4–6 SERVINGS

1. Sauté garlic in hot oil until fragrant. Add paneer, spices, and tomato paste and fry 5–6 minutes until everything is well blended.

2. Season with salt, and mix to blend well.

3. Pack each jalapeño half tightly with the paneer filling. Dip into beaten egg and then bread crumbs to coat on all sides.

4. Deep-fry in hot oil until golden and crisp. Serve this dish immediately, as it tastes best when warm and crisp. Any leftovers can be easily reheated in the oven.

Paneer is a traditional Indian cheese that does not melt at high heat. This enables the filling to hold tight within the jalapeño and not ooze out while frying. The paneer mixture may firm up once it begins to cool. If this happens, warm it in the microwave for a couple of seconds to make it soft and easy to pack into the jalapeños.

Cheese and Green Chile Corn Muffins

INGREDIENTS

$\frac{1}{2}$ cup buttermilk
2 large eggs
$\frac{1}{3}$ cup sour cream
1 4-ounce can diced green chiles
$\frac{1}{2}$ cup canned cream-style corn
1 cup all-purpose flour
1 tablespoon baking powder
1 teaspoon salt
$\frac{1}{2}$ cup light brown sugar
1 cup yellow cornmeal
$\frac{1}{2}$ cup (1 stick) butter, melted
1 cup shredded cheddar

YIELD: 12 MUFFINS

1. In a medium bowl, whisk together the buttermilk, eggs, sour cream, chiles, and cream-style corn.

2. In a large bowl, combine the dry ingredients.

3. Fold the buttermilk mixture into the dry mixture with a rubber spatula. When well blended, fold in the melted butter and the cheese.

4. Bake in a muffin tin at 350°F until golden brown and a toothpick inserted into the center comes out clean, 30–35 minutes.

Pickled Carrots
and Jalapeños

INGREDIENTS

5 cloves garlic
1 pound peeled carrots
2 tablespoons cooking oil
$^3/_4$ cup vinegar
5 bay leaves
5 peppercorns
$^1/_2$ teaspoon salt
$^3/_4$ cup water
$^1/_4$ cup pickled jalapeños with the canning juice

YIELD: 6 CUPS

1. Peel and chop the garlic cloves. Peel and cut
   the carrots on the diagonal about $^1/_4$ inch
   thick.

2. Heat the oil in a large pan and sauté the
   garlic and carrots 2–3 minutes.

3. Slowly add the vinegar, bay leaves,
   peppercorns, and salt and bring to a simmer,
   5 minutes.

4. Add the water and jalapeños and simmer
   an additional 10 minutes. Cool the mixture
   and store in the refrigerator overnight for
   maximum flavor.

You can add more jalapeños at any point to increase the heat level.

Posole

INGREDIENTS

1 tablespoon oil
1 whole onion, peeled and coarsely chopped
5 cloves garlic, peeled and diced
1 pound boneless pork roast cut into 4–5 pieces
6 quarts water

2 cups dried hominy
$\frac{1}{2}$ teaspoon salt
1 teaspoon cumin
$\frac{1}{2}$ teaspoon oregano
$\frac{1}{4}$ teaspoon ground cloves
$\frac{1}{4}$ teaspoon pepper
1 8-ounce can diced green chiles
1 jalapeño, seeded and finely diced

YIELD: 8 SERVINGS

1. Heat the oil in a large pot over medium heat. Add onion, garlic, and pork. Sauté until garlic becomes golden and pork begins to brown.

2. Add the water to the pot along with the dried hominy, salt, cumin, oregano, cloves, pepper, chiles, and jalapeños. Simmer 2 hours.

3. Remove pork from the liquid and cut into bite-size pieces; return meat to the soup.

4. Cook an additional 30–45 minutes, until hominy is tender.

Serve topped with chopped cilantro, chopped fresh Mexican oregano, and lime wedges or for a bolder addition, try chopped fresh onion, sliced radish, or chile sauce to spice up the flavor.

Guacamole Poblano

INGREDIENTS

2 poblano chiles
3 large ripe Hass avocados
1/4 cup white onion, peeled and finely chopped
2 tablespoons lemon juice
2 teaspoons hot chile sauce
1/4 cup fresh cilantro, finely chopped
1/4 teaspoon salt, or more to taste

YIELD: 4–6 SERVINGS

1. Roast the poblanos under the broiler or on a grill until the skins are black (see page 8).

2. Remove the skin, stems, and seeds and finely dice the chiles.

3. Cut the avocados in half, remove the seeds, and scrape the flesh into a bowl; begin to mash.

If you need to postpone serving this dish, place a piece of plastic wrap over the container, touching the surface of the guacamole. If the guacamole begins to brown, just scrape off the discolored area and discard.

4. Add remaining ingredients and continue to mash together until combined. Serve immediately to avoid oxidation.

Red Chile Salsa

INGREDIENTS

3 beefsteak tomatoes
½ onion, peeled
4 dried guajillo chiles
1 red bell pepper
1 cup cilantro leaves
4 garlic cloves, peeled
2 tablespoons oil
2 limes, juiced
1 tablespoon vinegar
1 teaspoon salt

YIELD: 4-6 SERVINGS

1. Coarsely chop the tomatoes, discarding the watery seed portion, and cut the onion into large chunks.

2. Rehydrate the guajillo chiles (see page 10) and cut into chunks.

3. Cut the stem off the bell pepper, remove the seeds, and cut into chunks.

4. Add all ingredients to a food processor and process a few seconds at a time until the ingredients are well combined. Serve with tortilla chips.

Guajillos are a great choice for this salsa because they have a rich, earthy flavor but are not overpowering. If guajillos are not available, there are other chiles that also make great salsa. Pasilla chiles are a bit more spicy and have a unique herb flavor. Other delicious chiles are the Anaheim and New Mexico chiles, which are milder than the guajillo but still delicious.

Salsa Verde

INGREDIENTS

12 tomatillos
4 Anaheim chiles
1 medium white onion
1 bunch cilantro
5 cloves garlic
1 teaspoon vegetable oil
1 tablespoon lime juice
Salt to taste
$\frac{1}{2}$ cup water, as needed

YIELD: 4–6 SERVINGS

1. Remove the husks from the tomatillos, rinse them thoroughly to remove the sticky residue, and then cut them into quarters.

2. Char the Anaheim chiles under a broiler or a grill and remove the skins (see page 8), seeds, and stems.

3. Coarsely chop the onion and cilantro.

4. Add all the ingredients except the water to a food processor and mix on low speed until ingredients are combined. Serve warm as a stew-type dish or lightly chilled or at room temperature as a condiment or topping.

Roasted Chile Salsa

INGREDIENTS

1 pound large, fresh red chiles such as Anaheim
1 red bell pepper
1 onion, cut into quarters
6 garlic cloves
1 pound ripe tomatoes
1 cup cilantro leaves
3 tablespoons vinegar
1 teaspoon salt

YIELD: 4-6 SERVINGS

1. Roast the chiles and bell pepper until the skins are blackened. Peel the skins off and remove the stems and seeds.

2. Place the onion quarters, garlic, and tomatoes onto a baking sheet and brown them under a broiler.

3. Let the tomatoes cool, cut the stem area out, and use a spoon to scoop out the majority of the seeds and liquid.

4. Place all the ingredients into a food processor and process until combined. Serve the salsa immediately, or let it rest in the refrigerator overnight so the flavors can blend.

If fresh red chiles are not available, substitute fresh green chiles such as New Mexico or poblano chiles. The green chiles will give the salsa a more muted neutral color rather than a bright red tone, but it will still have excellent flavor.

Jalapeño-Mango Salsa

INGREDIENTS

3 plum tomatoes
2 mangoes
1 jalapeño
$\frac{1}{2}$ small red onion
1 garlic clove
$\frac{1}{2}$ cup cilantro leaves
$\frac{1}{2}$ teaspoon of salt
$\frac{1}{2}$ teaspoon ground white pepper
1 tablespoon lemon juice
1 tablespoon olive oil

YIELD: 4–6 SERVINGS

1. Chop the tomatoes and discard the seeds.

2. Cut the mango off the seed and away from the skin in small chunks.

3. Cut the stem off the jalapeño and remove the seeds; finely dice.

4. Chop the onion, garlic, and cilantro.

5. Place all the ingredients in a large bowl and toss until combined. Place the salsa in an airtight container and refrigerate overnight to allow the flavors to fully incorporate.

Habañero Salsa

INGREDIENTS

4 large tomatoes
2 habañero chiles
2 jalapeño chiles
1 small red onion
3 garlic cloves
2 tablespoons lemon juice
½ teaspoon salt

YIELD: 6–8 SERVINGS

1. Seed and dice the tomatoes, discarding most of the seeds and pulp, and place them in a large bowl.

2. Roast chiles (see page 8), cut them in half, scrape out the seeds, and remove the stems.

3. Finely chop the chiles and add them to the tomatoes.

4. Dice the onion and garlic and add them to the mixture.

5. Sprinkle the lemon juice and salt over the top and fold the mixture to thoroughly incorporate it. Let the salsa rest in the refrigerator overnight so the flavors can fully blend. Let the salsa return to room

temperature before serving to allow the flavors to fully unfold.

Make sure to warn guests about the heat level of the salsa, as it may be overwhelming for some.

Roast Chicken with Onion and Chile

INGREDIENTS

3–4 tablespoons extra-virgin olive oil
1 small onion, cut into rings
2 garlic cloves, crushed

1 whole chicken, 2–3 pounds, cut into pieces
1 small chile pepper, finely chopped
Salt and freshly ground black pepper
1 tablespoon tomato paste
¾ cup dry white wine
A few sprigs of rosemary, with 1 sprig finely
  chopped
6–8 tablespoons chicken stock (low-sodium)

YIELD: 4 SERVINGS

1. Heat the oil in a casserole dish; sauté onion
   rings and crushed garlic for 5 minutes. Add
   chicken to casserole, followed by chile.
   Season to taste. Brown chicken on all sides
   over moderate heat.

2. Mix tomato paste with some warm water;
   add to casserole along with wine. Reduce
   heat, cover, and cook for approximately 30
   minutes.

3. Sprinkle chopped rosemary over chicken.
   Cook for 30 more minutes, or until tender,
   occasionally adding stock. Garnish with
   remaining sprigs of rosemary.

Chile-Lime Chicken

INGREDIENTS

3 dried chiles such as ancho or guajillo
2–3 cloves garlic, crushed or finely diced
3 tablespoons lime juice
1 jalapeño
5 boneless, skinless chicken breasts
4 limes, cut into slices
½ teaspoon salt

YIELD: 5 SERVINGS

1. Remove stems and seeds from the chiles and soak in warm water 30 minutes, until softened.

2. For the marinade, puree the chiles with the garlic, lime juice, and jalapeño. Add a little chile soaking liquid if it is too thick.

3. Place chicken, lime slices, and salt in a glass baking dish; add the marinade. Pierce each chicken breast with a fork, about 15–20 times.

4. Cover and refrigerate 30 minutes. Remove chicken from marinade and cook on a medium-hot grill until cooked through.

Chicken Verde

INGREDIENTS

1 (4-pound) whole chicken
1 onion, quartered
3 whole cloves garlic
2 teaspoons salt
Water to cover
2 tablespoons olive oil

1 onion, chopped
3 cloves garlic, minced
1 jalapeño pepper, minced
2 cups tomatillos, chopped
1 green bell pepper
$1/2$ cup salsa verde (see recipe on page 25)
$1/2$ cup chopped cilantro
$1/2$ teaspoon cumin

YIELD: 6 SERVINGS

1. Place chicken in pot. Add quartered onion, whole garlic, and salt; cover with water.

2. Simmer for $1\frac{1}{2}$ hours until chicken is tender. Remove and shred meat; discard skin and bones. Reserve broth.

3. In large saucepan, heat oil; cook chopped onion and minced garlic 4 minutes. Add jalapeño, tomatillos, bell pepper, green salsa, chicken, and 1 cup broth.

4. Bring to a simmer; add cilantro and cumin. Simmer 20-30 minutes until mixture is blended. Serve over rice or in enchiladas.

If you'd like a spicier sauce, use more jalapeño peppers, or add a habañero or dried ancho chile.

Chicken Fajitas

INGREDIENTS

3 tablespoons cider vinegar
2 tablespoons honey
1 teaspoon cumin
1 tablespoon red chile powder
1 tablespoon lime juice
$\frac{1}{2}$ teaspoon salt
3 cups cooked sliced or cubed chicken breast
2 tablespoons olive oil
2 red bell peppers
1 green bell pepper
1 red onion, chopped
8 (8-inch) flour tortillas
1 cup salsa
1 cup sour cream
2 avocados, peeled and sliced
1 cup shredded Pepper Jack cheese

YIELD: 4 SERVINGS

1. In bowl, combine vinegar, honey, cumin, chile powder, lime juice, and salt; add chicken and stir.

2. Cover and marinate in refrigerator 30 minutes. Then heat olive oil; add bell peppers and onion; cook 5–6 minutes until tender.

3. Add chicken mixture to bell peppers; cook and stir 3-4 minutes until heated. Meanwhile, wrap tortillas in foil; warm in 350°F oven 8-10 minutes.

4. Make fajitas with flour tortillas, chicken mixture, salsa, sour cream, avocados, and cheese.

For a party, place the tortillas and several types of filling on a warming tray, then let everyone assemble their own.

Chicken, Chile, and Cheese Flautas

INGREDIENTS

1½ cups shredded chicken
¾ cup shredded queso quesadilla (mild Mexican white cheese)
¼ cup diced, canned green chiles
¾ cup canned green chile sauce
Pinch of salt
10 flour tortillas
10 toothpicks for securing tortillas
3 tablespoons canola oil

YIELD: 5 SERVINGS

1. Toss the chicken, cheese, chiles, chile sauce, and salt in a bowl until evenly combined.

2. Place a tortilla on a flat surface and add 2 tablespoons chicken mixture in a straight line just off center.

3. Roll one edge of the tortilla over the filling and slightly under it. Roll it up the rest of the way and secure with a toothpick in the center. Repeat steps 2 and 3 until all tortillas are filled.

4. Fry flautas on both sides in oil until golden and crispy. Remove the toothpicks; serve immediately.

Chicken Mole

INGREDIENTS

1 dried ancho chile
1 dried pasilla chile
$1/2$ cup boiling water
2 tablespoons butter
2 pounds boneless, skinless chicken thighs
2 tablespoons flour
1 teaspoon salt
$1/8$ teaspoon pepper
1 onion, chopped
3 cloves garlic, minced
$1/3$ cup raisins, finely chopped
1 (8-ounce) can tomato sauce
$1/4$ cup peanut butter
2 teaspoons red chile powder
$1/2$ teaspoon cumin
$1/8$ teaspoon ground cloves
$1/2$ ounce unsweetened chocolate, chopped
$1 1/2$ cups chicken broth
$1/4$ cup chopped fresh cilantro

YIELD: 6 SERVINGS

1. Soak dried chiles in water 5 minutes; drain, then chop chiles. Discard stems.

2. Melt butter. Sprinkle chicken with flour, salt, and pepper; brown chicken 4 minutes. Remove from pan.

3. Add onion, garlic, chiles, and raisins to pan; cook and stir 4 minutes. Puree using immersion blender.

4. Stir in remaining ingredients except cilantro; bring to a simmer. Add chicken; simmer 40 minutes. Shred chicken and return to sauce. Serve over hot cooked rice with cilantro.

Enchiladas Verde

INGREDIENTS

12 corn tortillas
$1/2$ cup cooking oil
2 cups shredded chicken
1 29-ounce can green chile sauce
$1^1/2$ cups shredded or crumbled queso fresco or queso blanco
1 4-ounce can diced green chiles
$1/4$ cup crumbled Cotija cheese

YIELD: 4–6 SERVINGS

1. Lightly brush tortillas with cooking oil. Heat one on a comal, or griddle, over medium heat.

2. Remove warm tortilla and place chicken, a drizzle of chile sauce, and cheese down the center.

3. Roll tortilla around filling; place seam side down in 9x13-inch baking dish. Repeat with remaining tortillas, chicken, sauce, and cheese.

4. Pour remaining chile sauce over the top. Sprinkle with diced green chiles and any remaining cheese. Bake at 350°F for 35 minutes. Top with Cotija before serving.

Enchilada means "in chile," and the earliest enchiladas were simply a tortilla dipped in chile sauce and then rolled up and eaten. They have since evolved to include meats, cheeses, vegetables, and more.

Pollo Fundido

INGREDIENTS

Fundido Sauce:
4 ounces cream cheese
$\frac{1}{2}$ cup Crema Agria
$\frac{1}{2}$ cup heavy cream
1 garlic clove, crushed
1 jalapeño, seeds and stem removed

1 tablespoon oil
6 boneless, skinless chicken breasts
3 cloves garlic, crushed

½ cup chopped onion

1 bell pepper, chopped

1 stalk celery, chopped

¼ teaspoon cumin

½ teaspoon ground chile powder

½ teaspoon salt

¼ cup red chile sauce

10 medium flour tortillas

2 cups cooking oil

Fundido Sauce

1 cup grated queso Chihuahua or Manchego cheese

YIELD: 5 SERVINGS

1. Combine ingredients for Fundido Sauce into a blender. Pulse on low speed until well combined. Keep in refrigerator until ready to serve Pollo Fundido.

2. Heat the oil in a large saucepan over medium heat. Cut the chicken into bite-size pieces and cook 5 minutes.

3. Add the garlic, onion, vegetables, seasonings, and chile sauce; cook until the chicken is done and the vegetables have softened.

4. Roll the chicken filling into the tortillas and fry in hot oil until golden on each side.

5. Top with Fundido Sauce and grated cheese. Broil until the cheese is melted. Serve immediately.

Stuffed Peppers

INGREDIENTS

¼ pound fresh turkey sausage
1 tablespoon olive oil
2 cloves garlic, minced
½ cup chopped mushrooms
¾ cup cooked rice
½ teaspoon turmeric
¼ cup finely chopped fresh parsley
Sea salt and freshly ground pepper, to taste
2 bell peppers, tops cut off and seeded

YIELD: 2 SERVINGS

1. Slice open sausages and remove meat from
   the casings. In a skillet over medium-high
   heat, heat oil and toss in garlic. Add sausage
   and brown.

2. Remove meat from skillet; add mushrooms.
   Cook a few minutes, until soft, then return
   meat to skillet, stirring well.

3. Combine cooked rice with meat mixture. Add
   turmeric, parsley, and salt and pepper.

4. Add mixture to peppers. Bake in a 375°F
   preheated oven 25–30 minutes. Use tongs
   to gently place stuffed peppers onto serving
   dish.

To cut the top off the peppers, use a sharp chef's knife. Using a smaller paring knife, seed the peppers by removing the membranes and seeds. The peppers should be entirely hollow for stuffing.

Turkey Chili with Beans

INGREDIENTS

¼ cup olive or canola oil

1 pound ground turkey

4 yellow cooking onions, peeled and coarsely chopped

4 cloves garlic, smashed and chopped

3 green bell peppers, cored, seeded, and diced

1–2 serrano peppers OR 3 jalapeño peppers, chopped, seeds in for extra heat

1 sweet red pepper, cored, seeded, roasted and peeled (from a jar is fine)

2 teaspoons unsweetened cocoa powder

2 teaspoons dried thyme leaves

2 tablespoons chile powder, or to taste

1 teaspoon freshly ground black pepper

1 teaspoon salt

½ can (about 6 ounces) low-sodium beef broth

1 28-ounce can Italian plum tomatoes

6 ounces flat beer

1 pound red kidney beans, soaked overnight OR 4 cans red kidney beans, drained and rinsed

YIELD: 10 SERVINGS

1. Heat the olive oil in a large pot and lightly brown the turkey, then add the vegetables. Cook until the onions are translucent.

2. Stir in the cocoa powder, thyme, chile powder, pepper, and salt; mix well.

3. Add the liquids, tomatoes, and beans; stir to blend. Pour into slow cooker and cook on low for 4–6 hours. Or bake in the oven at 250°F for at least 3–4 hours.

Turkey Sausage with Onions and Peppers

INGREDIENTS

1 tablespoon olive oil, divided
4 spicy Italian-style turkey sausages, roughly 1
  pound

2 cloves garlic, minced
1 yellow onion, chopped
Sea salt and freshly ground pepper, to taste
1 red bell pepper, chopped
1 yellow bell pepper, chopped
2 bay leaves
Pinch of oregano

YIELD: 2 SERVINGS

1. Heat up oiled pan over medium-high heat. Sear sausages on all sides for a few minutes each.

2. Place sausages in a baking dish and cook 10–15 minutes in a 350°F preheated oven.

3. Heat up the rest of the oil and add the garlic, onions, and salt and pepper. Sauté until onions are soft.

4. Toss in peppers, bay leaves, and oregano and sauté another 5–8 minutes, until peppers have softened. Transfer sausages to the pan and cook 10 minutes, stirring once.

> If you can't find hot paprika, you can always substitute cayenne pepper.

Hunan Chile Beef
with Peppers

INGREDIENTS

1 pound flank steak, thinly sliced
3 tablespoons soy sauce, divided
2 tablespoons rice wine
1 teaspoon rice wine vinegar

1 teaspoon sugar
1 tablespoon cornstarch
5 fresh hot chiles, two or more colors
2–3 tablespoons vegetable oil
3 cloves garlic, minced
1 teaspoon grated ginger root
2 tablespoons fermented black beans, rinsed
1 teaspoon sesame oil
2 tablespoons cilantro, minced
Salt to taste

YIELD: 4–6 SERVINGS

1. Combine steak with 2 tablespoons soy sauce, wine, vinegar, and sugar. Add cornstarch and stir. Refrigerate 30 minutes.

2. Cut chiles into thin strips. Add 2 tablespoons oil to a hot wok. Add beef and cook without stirring 1 minute. Stir-fry beef 30 seconds and remove to a bowl.

3. Add more oil to wok. Stir-fry garlic, ginger, and chiles 1 minute. Add remaining soy sauce, black beans, and sesame oil.

4. Return beef to wok. Stir-fry 30 seconds. Add cilantro and salt. Serve immediately.

Braciola Stuffed with Peppers

INGREDIENTS

¼ cup low-sodium soy sauce

2 tablespoons packed light brown sugar

1 pound beef tenderloin

4 green onions, green tops only, cut into 3-inch pieces and sliced lengthwise

2 celery ribs, sliced very thin (¼- by 4-inch pieces)

1 red bell pepper and 1 yellow bell pepper, trimmed, seeded, and cut into ¼- by 4-inch pieces

2 tablespoons olive oil

Salt and black pepper, to taste

YIELD: 4 SERVINGS

1. Prepare the grill, or preheat the broiler. In a small bowl, whisk together the soy sauce and brown sugar until dissolved.

2. Trim the beef tenderloin into 8 slices, approximately ½ inch thick. Pound the beef with a meat mallet until ⅛ inch thick. Brush one side of each beef slice with the soy sauce mixture. Sprinkle with salt and pepper.

3. Distribute the vegetables equally on each piece of beef. Roll up lengthwise, and skewer each braciola with toothpicks to seal it tightly.

4. Grill or broil the beef rolls, brushing with oil to prevent sticking. Grill each roll until it's well browned and the vegetables are hot, about 5 minutes, turning once. The edges of the rolls will begin to curl after about 2$\frac{1}{2}$ minutes. Season with salt and pepper.

Italian Steak and Pepper Sandwiches

INGREDIENTS

¼ cup honey mustard

1 tablespoon horseradish

⅓ cup sour cream

½ teaspoon dried oregano leaves

½ teaspoon dried basil leaves

⅛ teaspoon pepper

4 hoagie buns, sliced

¼ cup butter, softened

2 leftover grilled rib eye steaks

1 (7-ounce) jar roasted red peppers

2 cups shredded provolone cheese

2 cups baby spinach or arugula leaves

YIELD: 4 SANDWICHES

1. Combine mustard, horseradish, sour cream, oregano, basil, and pepper.

2. Spread cut sides of hoagie buns with butter; grill until golden brown. Place on work surface.

3. Slice the steak against the grain. Drain peppers on paper towel; cut into thin strips. Spread buns with mustard mixture; layer on steak, cheese, peppers, spinach.

4. Top with hoagie bun tops. Wrap in foil. Grill sandwiches over medium direct heat, turning several times and pressing with spatula, for 9–12 minutes.

Steak-and-Pepper Quesadillas

INGREDIENTS

14-ounce top sirloin steak
¼ teaspoon salt
¼ teaspoon black pepper
1 lime, juiced

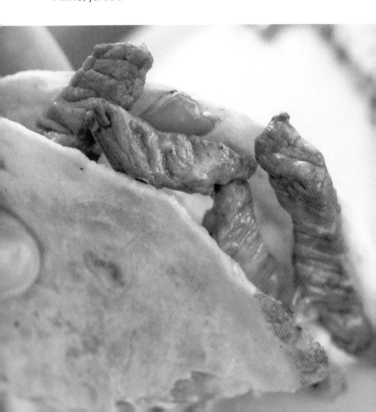

1 tablespoon oil
1 small red bell pepper
1 small green bell pepper
1 small white onion
$\frac{1}{2}$ teaspoon cumin
1 teaspoon ground chile
4 large flour tortillas
2 cups shredded Monterey Jack cheese, divided
$\frac{1}{4}$ cup red chile sauce

YIELD: 2 SERVINGS

1. Coat the steak with salt, pepper, and lime juice; grill over medium-high heat until only slightly pink inside. Let it cool slightly; slice into $\frac{1}{4}$-inch pieces.

2. Heat the oil in a saucepan over medium heat and sauté peppers, onion, and seasonings until softened.

3. Heat a tortilla on a comal over low heat. Add $\frac{1}{2}$ cup cheese, half the steak, half the pepper mixture, and top with remaining cheese and another tortilla. Heat until cheese is melted. Repeat with remaining ingredients. Add sauce and serve.

Carne Asada

INGREDIENTS

5–6 dried red chiles, stems and seeds removed
3 tablespoons fresh-squeezed lime juice
$\frac{1}{4}$ teaspoon cumin
Salt, to taste
2–3 pounds skirt steak

YIELD: 4–6 SERVINGS

1. Rehydrate and puree the dried chiles with the lime juice, cumin, and $\frac{1}{4}$ cup of the soaking liquid.

2. Prepare the steak, removing any excess membranes and fat. Place in a glass dish.

3. Soak chiles in hot water for 30 minutes and place in a food processor with $\frac{1}{4}$ cup soaking liquid, the lime juice, cumin, and salt. Process until all ingredients are well combined.

4. Pour the marinade over the steak and marinate in the refrigerator a minimum of 1 hour and up to 24 hours.

5. On a hot grill, sear the meat 2 minutes each side; reduce heat to medium and slowly cook until steak is medium well.

The type of chile used for the carne asada marinade can make a huge difference in the flavor and heat of carne asada. If you want a very mild and earthy flavor, New Mexico, California, or ancho chiles are great choices. For a spicier marinade, try pasilla chiles or add a piquin chile with the milder ones to spice it up.

Italian Sausage and Pepper Sandwiches

INGREDIENTS

$1/2$ cup beer
$1/4$ cup barbecue sauce
$1/3$ cup water
$1/2$ teaspoon salt
$1/8$ teaspoon pepper
10 dashes hot sauce
6 fresh sweet or hot Italian sausages
2 green bell peppers, sliced
1 cup sliced mushrooms
6 6-inch x 2-inch slices provolone cheese
6 sausage buns
$1/2$ cup barbecue sauce

YIELD: 6 SANDWICHES

1. In large saucepan, combine beer, barbecue sauce, water, salt, pepper, and hot sauce. Bring to a simmer over medium heat. Place on grill.

2. Add sausages and bring to a simmer. Cover pan; simmer for 8–9 minutes or until sausages are almost done.

3. Place sausages on direct heat; grill until fully cooked and nicely marked. Combine peppers

and mushrooms in grill basket; grill for 3–4 minutes.

4. When sausages are done, top with cheese. Grill buns. Assemble sandwiches.

Fresh sausages can be frozen when you get them home from the store. Wrap in freezer wrap or place in freezer bags. Label and freeze up to 6 months. To thaw, let stand in the refrigerator overnight; never thaw at room temperature. Cook the thawed sausages just as you would fresh ones.

Spanish-Style Pork Chops with Peppers

INGREDIENTS

2 tablespoons red wine vinegar
2 tablespoons olive oil
3 cloves garlic, minced

1 teaspoon salt
¼ teaspoon white pepper
½ teaspoon dried oregano leaves
6 thin boneless pork chops
3 slices bacon
1 onion, chopped
1 cup chicken stock
1 (8-ounce) can tomato sauce
2 teaspoons chile powder
2 red bell peppers, sliced
1 green bell pepper, sliced

YIELD: 6 SERVINGS

1. Mix vinegar, olive oil, garlic, salt, pepper, and oregano. Add pork chops; cover; chill for 3–4 hours.

2. When ready to eat, cook bacon in cast iron skillet on grill until crisp; remove and drain. Add onion; cook until tender, then add chicken stock, tomato sauce, and chile powder; simmer.

3. Place peppers in grill basket. Drain chops, discarding marinade. Grill over direct medium heat until peppers are tender and chops register 150°F.

4. Add to skillet on grill; simmer 2–3 minutes to blend flavors. Serve over hot cooked rice or couscous.

Chili Verde

INGREDIENTS

3 tablespoons oil
1$\frac{1}{2}$ pounds boneless pork loin, cut into 2-inch
cubes
2 cups chicken broth
1 cup green chile sauce
1 medium onion, peeled and diced
4 garlic cloves, peeled and diced
2 cups tomatillos, husks removed and coarsely
chopped
2 poblano chiles, roasted
$\frac{1}{4}$ teaspoon black pepper
$\frac{1}{2}$ teaspoon salt
$\frac{1}{2}$ teaspoon ground cumin
$\frac{1}{2}$ teaspoon sugar

YIELD: 4–6 SERVINGS

1. Heat oil in a skillet over high heat; quickly
   brown the outside of the pork.

2. Pour the broth and chile sauce into a large
   pot and bring to a boil.

3. Add the pork, onion, garlic, and tomatillos;
   simmer 2 hours over low heat. Meanwhile,
   roast the chiles (see page 8).

4. Add the chiles and let them simmer another
   hour. The liquid should reduce to a thin

sauce. Season with pepper, salt, cumin, and sugar.

The type of chile used in this recipe plays an important role in the flavor of the final dish. The dark green poblano has a fresh, grassy flavor with mild heat. The light green hatch chile has an earthier taste with medium heat. If you can't locate fresh green chiles, substitute with canned, which are already roasted and peeled and ready to use.

Chiles en Nogada

INGREDIENTS

Walnut Sauce:
½ bolillo roll (Mexican savory bread)
1 cup whole milk
½ cup heavy cream
¼ cup cream cheese
½ pound shelled and peeled fresh walnuts
1 tablespoon honey
Cinnamon and salt, to taste

6 poblano chiles
½ pound ground pork
3 cloves garlic
¼ cup white onion, chopped
1 green apple, peeled, cored, and chopped
¼ cup crushed pineapple
2 tablespoons raisins, softened in warm water
¼ teaspoon each cinnamon, nutmeg, and cumin
3 eggs, separated
Salt to taste
½ cup cooking oil
Walnut Sauce
1 pomegranate, seeds removed
1 bunch parsley

YIELD: 6 SERVINGS

1. To make Walnut Sauce, tear bolillo roll into chunks and place in a blender with remaining

ingredients. Pulse on high speed until sauce is smooth.

2. Char, peel, and deseed the poblano chiles (see page 8).

3. Brown the pork with the garlic, onion, apple, pineapple, raisins, and seasonings. Stuff chiles once filling cools slightly.

4. Whip the egg whites into stiff peaks; fold in the yolks and salt until a batter forms.

5. Dip each chile in the batter and fry on each side until golden brown. Top with Walnut Sauce, pomegranate seeds, and parsley, and serve.

Christmas Stuffed Peppers

INGREDIENTS

3 large ripe tomatoes
½ pound sweet Italian sausage
1 cup cooked ham
1 medium yellow onion, finely chopped
2 large eggs, lightly beaten

⅓–½ cup milk
¼ teaspoon ground nutmeg, preferably fresh
1 teaspoon seasoned salt
¼–½ teaspoon coarsely ground pepper
⅓ cup grated Romano or Parmesan cheese, divided
1 cup fine dry bread crumbs, divided
3 red bell peppers, seeded and parboiled
3 green bell peppers, seeded and parboiled

YIELD: 6 SERVINGS

1. Plunge the tomatoes into boiling water for 30 seconds. Drain and rinse under cold running water. Slip off skins and mash roughly with a fork.

2. In a mixing bowl, mash the sausage meat with the ham, onion and tomatoes. If using sausage in a casing, cut at the end and squeeze the meat out.

3. Blend in the eggs, milk, seasonings, half the cheese, and half the bread crumbs.

4. Stuff the peppers with the filling, sprinkle with the remaining cheese and bread crumbs, and bake in a greased gratin dish at 375°F for 30 minutes.

5. Decorate the peppers with mashed potato "elf hats" using a pastry bag with a ½-inch fluted tip and about 3 cups mashed potatoes.

Hot and Sour Pork Tenderloin

INGREDIENTS

¼ cup olive oil
3 tablespoons soy sauce
3 tablespoons hoisin sauce
2 tablespoons hot mustard
Juice of ½ lime
2 cloves garlic, minced
2 tablespoons grated fresh ginger
1 1-pound pork tenderloin
1 yellow bell pepper, roughly chopped
1 red bell pepper, roughly chopped

YIELD: 5 SERVINGS

1. In a shallow bowl, combine the olive oil, soy sauce, hoisin sauce, hot mustard, lime juice, garlic, and ginger, and whisk together until smooth.

2. Marinate the tenderloin in this mixture for 20 minutes or more.

3. In a large pan over medium-high heat, sear the tenderloin on each side for 5–6 minutes.

4. Arrange the bell peppers around the tenderloin and, in an oven preheated to 375°F, cook for 15–18 minutes, or until a little pink inside. Remove the tenderloin from the pan and place it on a cutting board to cool.

Slice it diagonally and serve 2–3 slices per person with the peppers over the top.

In this recipe the pork is sweetened with hoisin sauce, also called "suckling pig sauce," a concoction of sugar, soybeans, white distilled vinegar, rice, salt, flour, garlic, and red chile peppers used in Chinese cooking. You can also kick up the heat in this recipe by tossing in some hot peppers. A little spice can be nice!

Crispy Carp with Chiles

INGREDIENTS

1 2-pound whole carp or other whole fish,
  cleaned and scaled
Salt and pepper
4 tablespoons cornstarch
Vegetable oil for frying

4 cloves garlic, minced
2 tablespoons grated ginger root
6 fresh chile peppers, cored and sliced
2 green onions, sliced
2 tablespoons fermented black beans, rinsed
2 tablespoons soy sauce
1 tablespoon rice wine
1 teaspoon sesame oil
1 teaspoon sugar
2 tablespoons chopped cilantro

YIELD: 4 SERVINGS

1. Rinse fish well, then pat dry. Make two or three shallow cuts in each side of the fish.

2. Sprinkle with salt and pepper, then dust with cornstarch until well coated.

3. Heat a wok over high heat. Add vegetable oil to a depth of 3 inches. When oil is hot, add fish and fry 6–8 minutes per side. Place the fish on a platter.

4. Remove all but 1 tablespoon oil from wok. Return wok to high heat. Add garlic, ginger, peppers, and green onions. Stir-fry 2 minutes.

5. Combine black beans, soy sauce, wine, sesame oil, and sugar. Add to wok and stir-fry another minute. Pour sauce and peppers over the fish and garnish with chopped cilantro.

Salmon with Sweet Pepper Sauce

INGREDIENTS

Sweet Pepper Sauce:
2 red bell peppers, roasted, peeled, and seeded
  (available by the jar in supermarkets)
2 garlic cloves, finely chopped
3 tablespoons freshly squeezed lemon juice
$1/2$ cup low-fat mayonnaise
1 pinch cayenne pepper
1 teaspoon chile powder
1 teaspoon honey

2 tablespoons olive oil
2 tablespoons freshly ground black pepper
4 (6-ounce) salmon steaks

YIELD: 4 SERVINGS

1. Preheat the broiler.

2. In a food processor or blender, combine the peppers, garlic, lemon juice, mayonnaise, cayenne pepper, chile powder, and honey.

3. Mix on high speed for 30 seconds or with a hand blender for 1–2 minutes until blended well. Set aside.

4. Pour the oil onto a plate. Place the black pepper on another plate. Dip the salmon in the oil, then press it into the pepper.

5. Broil the salmon, turning once after 4 minutes for medium-rare. When the salmon sweats, the fish is done.

6. Serve with Sweet Pepper Sauce for dipping on the side, approximately 2 tablespoons per serving.

SEAFOOD

Fiery Shrimp

INGREDIENTS

2 ancho chiles, dried
1 chile de arbol, dried
$1/2$ cup tomato sauce
4 garlic cloves, peeled and crushed
$1/4$ cup chopped onion
1 lime, juiced
1 teaspoon white vinegar
2 tablespoons cooking oil
$1/4$ teaspoon salt (or more to taste)
25 large frozen shrimp, thawed, shelled and
   cleaned
1 green onion, chopped

YIELD: 2–3 SERVINGS

1. Cut the stems off of the dried chiles and slit
   them down the side. Shake them to remove
   the seeds.

2. Soak the chiles in hot water 30 minutes.
   Reserve $1/2$ cup soaking liquid.

3. In a blender, puree the chiles, tomato sauce,
   garlic, onion, lime juice, vinegar, oil, and salt
   into a sauce.

4. Place 5 shrimp on each skewer; baste with
   sauce. Grill over medium heat until done.

While this dish is meant to be extremely spicy, you can tone down the heat by eliminating the chile de arbol which is the greatest source of heat. The ancho chiles are a bit spicy on their own, so you will still have some fiery flavor without being overpowering.

Tex-Mex Shrimp Kabobs

INGREDIENTS

1/4 cup red chile sauce
1/4 cup salsa
3 tablespoons honey
Salt and pepper to taste
1 1/2 pounds medium raw shrimp
1 each red and green bell pepper
1 onion, cut into 16 wedges
1 (8-ounce) package mushrooms

YIELD: 4 SERVINGS

1. In large bowl, combine chile sauce, salsa, honey, and salt and pepper. Add shrimp, bell pepper, onion, and mushrooms and toss to coat.

2. Cover and refrigerate for 15–20 minutes. Drain shrimp and vegetables, reserving marinade. Preheat broiler.

3. Thread shrimp and vegetables on metal skewers. Spray broiler pan with cooking spray; place kabobs on pan.

4. Broil 6 inches from heat for 5–7 minutes, turning once and brushing with reserved marinade, until shrimp curl and turn pink and vegetables are crisp-tender.

SEAFOOD

Asparagus with Scallops in Chili Sauce

INGREDIENTS

1 pound fresh asparagus
1 tablespoon butter
1 tablespoon vegetable oil
2 teaspoons chopped garlic
4 scallions, chopped
1 teaspoon grated fresh ginger
1 pound bay scallops
½ teaspoon salt
Finely grated zest and juice of 1 lime
1 small red chile, finely chopped
1 tablespoon Thai chile paste
Lime wedges

YIELD: 4 SERVINGS

1. Trim the tough ends off the asparagus and cut it into 1-inch pieces.

2. Heat the butter and oil in a skillet or wok. Stir-fry the garlic, scallions, and ginger for 1 minute. Do not brown.

3. Add the asparagus and scallops and continue stir-frying 4–5 minutes on high heat. Stir in the salt, lime zest, lime juice, chile, and chile paste.

4. Serve garnished with lime wedges and freshly cooked jasmine or basmati rice.

Although this recipe calls for a fresh chile pepper, it's not really a very hot dish. It uses only one small red chile and tempers that with mild chile paste. If you prefer your food hotter, rev it up with two chiles or add more chile paste. On the other hand, if you're not into the burn, you can always use a milder chile and add a little brown sugar.

Stir-Fried Salmon with Peppers and Nectarines

INGREDIENTS

1¼ cups orange juice
2 tablespoons cornstarch
¼ cup orange marmalade
1 tablespoon soy sauce
3 tablespoons honey
½ teaspoon salt
⅛ teaspoon pepper
1 pound salmon fillet, skin removed
1 onion, chopped
2 green bell peppers, sliced
2 nectarines, sliced
2 tablespoons peanut oil

YIELD: 4 SERVINGS

1. In medium bowl, combine the first ingredients. Cut salmon into 1-inch cubes and add to marinade.

2. Meanwhile, prepare onion, peppers, and nectarines. Heat oil in large skillet or wok over medium-high heat.

3. Add onion; stir-fry for 3 minutes. Drain salmon, reserving marinade. Add salmon with bell peppers to skillet; stir-fry for 3 minutes.

4. Stir marinade and add to skillet along with nectarines; stir-fry for 3–5 minutes until salmon is cooked and sauce has thickened. Serve over hot cooked rice.

Grilled Fish Kabobs

INGREDIENTS

1 tablespoon olive oil
4 cloves garlic, minced
$1/4$ cup minced red onion
2 tablespoons grated ginger root
$1/4$ teaspoons ground ginger
2 tablespoons lemon juice
1 teaspoon grated lemon zest
$1/8$ teaspoon cayenne pepper
$11/4$ pounds halibut steak
1 (8-ounce) package whole small mushrooms
4 green onions, cut into 2-inch pieces
2 red bell peppers, sliced

YIELD: 6 SERVINGS

1. In small saucepan cook garlic and onion in olive oil 4 minutes. Add ginger root; cook 3 minutes longer.

2. Remove from heat; add ground ginger, lemon juice, zest, and pepper. Place in glass baking dish.

3. Cut halibut into $11/4$-inch cubes; add to marinade; toss. Cover; chill 4–5 hours.

4. Prepare and preheat grill; place grill mat on rack. Thread fish, mushrooms, green onion,

and bell peppers on 8 metal skewers. Grill, brushing with marinade, 8–12 minutes, until done.

Red Pepper Eggplant Parmesan

INGREDIENTS

1 medium yellow onion, chopped
6 ounces sliced fresh mushrooms
$\frac{1}{2}$ cup plus 2 tablespoons olive oil, divided
2 teaspoons minced garlic
1 6-ounce can tomato paste
1 cup water
1 cup vegetable bouillon
1 cup red wine
1 28-ounce can diced tomatoes
1 tablespoon sugar
2 tablespoons fresh parsley
1 tablespoon each fresh basil and fresh oregano
2 bay leaves

$^1/_2$ teaspoon onion powder
1 teaspoon seasoned salt
$^1/_2$ teaspoon pepper
2 eggplants, cut crosswise into $^1/_2$-inch slices
Kosher salt as needed
2 medium red bell peppers, roasted and sliced
$1^1/_2$ cups shredded mozzarella
$1^1/_2$ cups shredded or grated Parmesan

YIELD: 8-12 SERVINGS

1. Sauté onion and mushrooms in 2 tablespoons olive oil for 2-3 minutes. Add garlic and brown for 20 seconds. Stir in tomato paste, water, bouillon, wine, tomatoes, sugar, and seasonings. Simmer 20 minutes.

2. Generously sprinkle eggplant with kosher salt and let sit for 1 hour. Rinse and blot dry with paper towels.

3. Sauté eggplant slices in the $^1/_2$ cup of olive oil in batches until browned. Drain.

4. Cover the bottom of a deep baking dish with $^1/_3$ of the marinara sauce (discard the bay leaves) and arrange half of eggplant over sauce. Cover with another $^1/_3$ of sauce, a layer of roasted pepper slices, and half the cheeses. Repeat and bake at 350°F for 30-40 minutes, until cheese is brown and bubbling.

Mixed Grilled Peppers

INGREDIENTS

2 green bell peppers
2 red bell peppers
1 yellow bell pepper
2 poblano peppers
2 pepperocinis
1/4 cup olive oil
1 tablespoon lime juice
1 teaspoon salt
1/4 teaspoon pepper

YIELD: 6 SERVINGS

1. Cut all the peppers in half; remove stems, tops, and seeds. In small bowl, combine remaining ingredients.

2. Combine peppers in 2 large resealable plastic bags. Pour half of the oil mixture into each bag.

3. Seal bag and gently knead to coat the peppers with the oil mixture. Let stand for 10 minutes.

4. Prepare grill for medium direct heat. Grill peppers, skin side down, turning occasionally, until skin is blistered and brown. Remove peppers from grill. You can remove the skin or leave it on.

Sweet peppers, such as bell peppers, will become sweeter when grilled. The heat of hot peppers like habañeros will decrease slightly when grilled, but they will still be very spicy.

Roasted Veggie Sandwiches

INGREDIENTS

1 red bell pepper, sliced
1 green bell pepper, sliced
1 yellow bell pepper, sliced
1 yellow summer squash, sliced
1 red onion, sliced
3 portobello mushrooms, sliced
2 tablespoons olive oil
2 tablespoons lemon juice
$1/4$ teaspoon pepper
1 teaspoon dried tarragon
1 teaspoon dried thyme
$1/4$ cup chopped parsley
6 French bread rolls
6 slices fresh mozzarella

YIELD: 6 SERVINGS

1. Preheat oven to 425°F. Place bell peppers, squash, onion, and mushrooms on a roasting pan.

2. Drizzle with olive oil, lemon juice, and pepper; toss to coat. Roast 8–11 minutes, until vegetables are tender, turning once with spatula.

3. Add tarragon, thyme, and parsley and mix gently. Let cool 20 minutes. Layer vegetables and juices on split rolls.

VEGETARIAN

4. Top with mozzarella cheese, press together, and wrap in plastic wrap. Refrigerate 3–4 hours before serving.

A sturdy bread is necessary for this sandwich, otherwise it will fall apart after being refrigerated. Don't refrigerate the sandwiches longer than 4 hours or the bread will become soggy.

Chiles Rellenos

INGREDIENTS

8 poblano chiles
8 ¼-inch slices queso fresco cheese, about the
  height and width of the chiles
4 large eggs, separated
Pinch salt
1 cup cooking oil

YIELD: 4 SERVINGS

1. Char and peel the poblano chiles. Cut a
   small slit near the top of each chile and use a
   spoon to scrape out the seeds.

2. Place a cheese slice into each chile.

Even though most green chiles are ready to
pick at the end of summer, you can usually
find them year-round. They are also easily grown in your own backyard and can be
found at most farmer's markets. Look for
chiles that are a uniform dark green color
that are firm to the touch. They should not
have any dark spots, dents, or tears, and they
should be free of any mold or wrinkled skin.

3. Whip the egg whites into stiff peaks and then fold in the yolks and salt until a batter forms.

4. Dip each chile into the egg batter and fry in oil until golden. Drain each chile and serve immediately.

Rajas con Crema

INGREDIENTS

8 poblano or New Mexico chiles
1/2 teaspoon cooking oil
1 small onion, thinly sliced
2 garlic cloves, peeled and diced
1/4 cup cilantro leaves
1 teaspoon oregano
1/4 cup Crema Agria (see Glossary)

YIELD: 4–6 SERVINGS

1. Roast the chiles over an open flame or under a broiler until the skins are charred. Peel them, remove the seeds, and cut them into strips; set aside.

2. Heat the oil in a large saucepan and sauté the onion 10 minutes.

3. Add the garlic, cilantro, and oregano and sauté 3 more minutes.

4. Remove from heat and stir in the Crema Agria to coat the vegetables. Serve with a stack of warm flour or corn tortillas and additional onions and cilantro as garnishes.

Four-Pepper Chili

INGREDIENTS

2 onions, chopped
4 cloves garlic, minced
1 jalapeño pepper, minced
1 red bell pepper, cut in half
1 green bell pepper, cut in half
1 poblano chile pepper, cut in half
1 (15-ounce) can black beans, drained
1 (15-ounce) can red beans, drained
1 (15-ounce) can white beans, drained
2 cups vegetable broth
2 tablespoons chile powder
1 teaspoon salt
¼ teaspoon pepper
1 teaspoon dried oregano
1 teaspoon dried marjoram
1 bay leaf

YIELD: 6 SERVINGS

1. Place onion and garlic in 4- or 5-quart slow cooker. Preheat broiler.

2. Place peppers on broiler rack, skin side up. Broil for 7–8 minutes until skin browns. Remove and wrap in foil; let steam 5 minutes. Remove and discard skins.

3. Chop peppers and add to slow cooker along with all remaining ingredients.

4. Cover and cook on low for 7–8 hours until chili is thickened. Remove bay leaf and thicken with cornstarch slurry, if needed; serve.

Three-Pepper Pesto Strata

INGREDIENTS

1 onion, chopped
2 tablespoons butter
3 bell peppers, assorted colors, sliced
1/2 cup shredded carrots
1 (7-ounce) package basil pesto
14 slices sourdough bread
1 cup shredded Havarti cheese
8 eggs
1 (12-ounce) can evaporated milk
1 tablespoon flour
Salt and pepper to taste

YIELD: 6-8 SERVINGS

1. Cook onion in butter over medium heat for 4 minutes. Add bell peppers and carrots and remove from heat.

2. Spread pesto on bread, then cut bread into cubes. Layer 1/3 each bread, vegetable mixture, and cheese in 5-quart slow cooker; repeat twice.

3. Beat eggs with milk, salt, and pepper; pour into slow cooker.

4. Cover and refrigerate for 6–8 hours. Then cook on low for 6–8 hours until strata is puffed and meat thermometer reads 165°F. Let stand 5 minutes, then serve.

Paneer with Peppers and Onions

INGREDIENTS

2 tablespoons vegetable oil
1 teaspoon cumin seeds
1 medium onion, sliced
1 teaspoon minced garlic
$1/2$ teaspoon red chile powder
$1/4$ teaspoon turmeric powder
$1/2$ teaspoon coriander powder
$1/2$ teaspoon garam masala powder
1 tablespoon tomato paste
1 block paneer, cut into bite-size cubes
1 green bell pepper, sliced
Salt, to taste

YIELD: 3-4 SERVINGS

1. Heat oil in a nonstick wok and sauté cumin seeds, onions, and garlic for a few minutes until onions are lightly browned.

2. Stir in spice powders and tomato paste and fry until fragrant.

3. Add paneer and peppers, season with salt, and stir-fry for a few minutes until paneer is cooked through and well coated with the spices, about 5-6 minutes.

To increase the heat level of this recipe, add 2-3 thinly sliced fresh jalapeños along with the peppers. As the dish cooks, the heat from the jalapeños will penetrate through it and impart their heat. You can also increase the amount of red chile powder to make this dish much spicier.

Red Pepper Cream Sauce

INGREDIENTS

Olive oil to coat
4 red bell peppers
1/4 cup (1/2 stick) butter
2 garlic cloves, minced
1 cup heavy cream or half-and-half
1 teaspoon grated nutmeg
1 1/2 teaspoons salt
1/4 teaspoon freshly grated black pepper
1/4 cup minced fresh basil

YIELD: 3 CUPS

1. Roast the peppers (see page 8).

2. Puree the roasted peppers in a food processor until smooth. Set aside.

3. In a large frying pan, heat the butter, and sauté the garlic over medium heat until soft. Add the pepper puree and mix well. Reduce the heat and gradually stir in the heavy cream. Add the nutmeg, salt, and pepper; cook, stirring, for 5 minutes. Remove from the heat, and stir in the basil.

4. Serve immediately, or refrigerate for up to 3 days.

5. Serve over pasta or as a dipping sauce for lobster.

When you're planning to roast peppers, shop for those that have a smooth bottom and thick walls. These are the easiest to peel.

Roasted Red Pepper Soup

INGREDIENTS

4 red bell peppers, cut in half
2 tomatoes, cut in half
1 onion, chopped
2 cloves garlic, minced

2 tablespoons butter

1 tablespoon olive oil

$1/2$ teaspoon salt

$1/8$ teaspoon pepper

4 cups vegetable broth, homemade or store-bought

1 teaspoon dried basil

2 tablespoons lemon juice

$1/3$ cup chopped fresh basil

$1/3$ cup grated Romano cheese or soy cheese

YIELD: 6 SERVINGS

1. Place peppers and tomatoes, skin side up, on broiling rack. Broil 6–9 minutes, turning occasionally, until deep brown.

2. Let cool 20 minutes, peel and discard skins. Then chop.

3. In pot cook onion and garlic in butter and olive oil 5 minutes. Add salt, pepper, broth, dried basil, and bell peppers and tomatoes.

4. Simmer 10 minutes. Puree with an immersion blender. Add lemon juice; garnish with fresh basil and cheese.

VEGETARIAN

Warm Lentil and Pepper Salad

INGREDIENTS

2 cups dried lentils, rinsed
$1/2$ cup water
$1/4$ cup red wine vinegar
4 tablespoons olive oil
1 teaspoon prepared mustard
1 teaspoon Worcestershire sauce
Juice of $1/2$ lemon
Salt and pepper to taste
$1/2$ cup sweet roasted red pepper, diced
4 cups napa cabbage, rinsed and shredded
Optional garnish: $1/2$ cup pitted and chopped
  Greek or Italian olives, 2 tablespoons capers,
  OR 1 tablespoon green peppercorns

YIELD: 4 SERVINGS

1. Over medium heat, cook the lentils in enough
   water to cover for 30 minutes.

2. In a bowl, whisk together $1/4$ cup vinegar,
   olive oil, mustard, Worcestershire sauce, and
   lemon juice.

3. Drain the lentils and place in a large bowl; add the dressing, salt, pepper, and roasted red peppers.

4. Divide the cabbage among serving plates. Arrange the lentils over the cabbage, and garnish as desired.

BOOKS

DeWitt, Dave. *The Chile Pepper Encyclopedia: Everything You'll Ever Need To Know About Hot Peppers,* William Morrow Cookbooks, 1999.
An alphabetical guide to chile peppers, along with essays and recipes.

DeWitt, Dave, and Paul Bosland. *The Complete Chile Pepper Book: A Gardener's Guide to Choosing, Growing, Preserving, and Cooking,* Timber Press, 2009.
A detailed look at all things chile pepper, written by one of the foremost experts on the subject.

Miller, Mark, and John Harrisson. *The Great Chile Book,* Ten Speed Press, 1991.

A great resource book featuring delicious recipes, full-color photos, and descriptions of 100 chiles.

WEB SITES

AllRecipes.com
http://allrecipes.com
This site features reader-submitted recipes that are rated by members. Recipes can be filtered by ingredient using the search feature.

Bon Appétit
www.bonappetit.com
Always features a variety of dishes with a unique spin on everyday ingredients like peppers.

The Chile Pepper Institute
http://aces.nmsu.edu/chilepepperinstitute
Affiliated with the New Mexico State University, this nonprofit organization will answer all of your chile-related questions. You can also purchase books, seeds, and merchandise from their Chile Shop.

Cooks.com

www.cooks.com

Any and all recipes, vegetable and otherwise, along with many tips, nutrition facts, and forums.

Epicurious

www.epicurious.com

Find virtually any pepper recipe here, with helpful slideshows and commentary.

Food Network

www.foodnetwork.com

Like the TV shows, the Web site for the food network is packed with information, from recipes to techniques.

Whole Foods Market

www.wholefoodsmarket.com/recipes

Search for delicious pepper recipes and new inspirations for using your favorite ingredient ●

APPROXIMATE U.S.-METRIC EQUIVALENTS

LIQUID INGREDIENTS

U.S. Measures	Metric	U.S. Measures	Metric
$\frac{1}{4}$ tsp.	1.23 ml	2 Tbsp.	29.57 ml
$\frac{1}{2}$ tsp.	2.36 ml	3 Tbsp.	44.36 ml
$\frac{3}{4}$ tsp.	3.70 ml	$\frac{1}{4}$ cup	59.15 ml
1 tsp.	4.93 ml	$\frac{1}{2}$ cup	118.30 ml
$1\frac{1}{4}$ tsp.	6.16 ml	1 cup	236.59 ml
$1\frac{1}{2}$ tsp.	7.39 ml	2 cups or 1 pt.	473.18 ml
$1\frac{3}{4}$ tsp.	8.63 ml	3 cups	709.77 ml
2 tsp.	9.86 ml	4 cups or 1 qt.	946.36 ml
1 Tbsp.	14.79 ml	4 qts. or 1 gal.	3.79 l

DRY INGREDIENTS

U.S. Measures	Metric	U.S. Measures	Metric
$\frac{1}{16}$ oz.	2 (1.8) g	$2\frac{4}{5}$ oz.	80 g
$\frac{1}{8}$ oz.	$3\frac{1}{2}$ (3.5) g	3 oz.	85 (84.9) g
$\frac{1}{4}$ oz.	7 (7.1) g	$3\frac{1}{2}$ oz.	100 g
$\frac{1}{2}$ oz.	15 (14.2) g	4 oz.	115 (113.2) g
$\frac{3}{4}$ oz.	21 (21.3) g	$4\frac{1}{2}$ oz.	125 g
$\frac{7}{8}$ oz.	25 g	$5\frac{1}{4}$ oz.	150 g
1 oz.	30 (28.3) g	$8\frac{7}{8}$ oz.	250 g
$1\frac{3}{4}$ oz.	50 g	16 oz. or 1 lb.	454 g
2 oz.	60 (56.6) g	$17\frac{3}{5}$ oz. or 1 livre	500 g

Broil: To cook food close to the heat source, quickly.

Capsaicin: The chemical found in peppers which causes a burning sensation when in contact with the eyes or mouth.

Chop: To cut food into small pieces, using a chef's knife or a food processor.

Comal: A type of griddle typically used in Mexican cooking.

Crema Agria: Mexican fresh cream dressing similar to sour cream. It is often used as a garnish or ingredient.

Grill: To cook over coals or charcoal, or over high heat.

Marinate: To allow meats or vegetables to stand in a mixture of an acid and oil, to add flavor and tenderize.

Paneer: A fresh Indian cheese that can easily be made at home and cooked without melting into the dish.

Parboil: To partially cook food by first boiling it.

Sauté: To cook food briefly in oil over medium-high heat, while stirring it so it cooks evenly.

Seasoning: To add herbs, spices, citrus juices and zest, and peppers to food to increase flavor.

Slow cooker: An appliance that cooks food by surrounding it with low, steady heat.

Stir-fry: To quickly cook food by manipulating it with a spoon or spatula, in a wok or pan, over high heat.

Toss: To combine food using two spoons or a spoon and a fork until mixed well.

Wok: A round-bottomed pan, typically used for stir-frying, popular in China ●